Action Art

Sculpting

Isabel Thomas

Heinemann Library
Chicago, Illinois

© 2005 Heinemann Library
a division of Reed Elsevier Inc.
Chicago, Illinois

Customer Service 888-454-2279

Visit our website at www.heinemannlibrary.com

Printed and bound in China by South China Printing Company Limited
Photo research by Mica Brancic

09 08 07 06 05
10 9 8 7 6 5 4 3 2 1

Library of Congress Cataloging-in-Publication Data
Thomas, Isabel, 1980-
   Action art : sculpting / Isabel Thomas.
        p. cm. -- (Action art)
   Includes bibliographical references and index.
   ISBN 1-4034-6921-0 (library binding-hardcover) -- ISBN 1-4034-6927-X (pbk.)
 1. Sculpture--Technique--Juvenile literature. I. Title. II. Series.
   NB1170.T47 2005
   731.4--dc22
                                                          2005001580

Acknowledgments
The author and publishers are grateful to the following for permission to reproduce
copyright material: Corbis pp. **13**, **15**; Getty p. **4**; Harcourt Education p. **14**
(Gareth Boden) p. **11** (Martin Sookias) p. **6** (Trevor Clifford), pp. **5**, **8**, **9**, **10**, **12**, **16**,
18, **19**, **20**, **21**, **22**, **23**, **24** (Tudor Photography); Topfoto pp. **7**, **17** (The Image Works)

Cover photograph of boy making a clay helicopter reproduced with permission of
Corbis/Gallo Images (Anthony Bannister)

Every effort has been made to contact copyright holders of any material reproduced in
this book. Any omissions will be rectified in subsequent printings if notice is given to
the publisher.

Many thanks to the teachers, library media specialists, reading instructors, and educational
consultants who have helped develop the Read and Learn/Lee y aprende brand.

Some words are shown in bold, **like this.** You can
find them in the picture glossary on page 23.

Contents

What Is Art?

Art is something you make when you are being **creative**.

People like to look at art.

A person who makes art is called an artist.

You can be an artist, too!

How Can
I Make Art?

There are lots of ways to make art.

You can draw and paint pictures.

Try making sculptures and collage with interesting **textures**.

What Are Sculptures?

Sculptures are not flat like paintings and drawings.

They are **three-dimensional.**

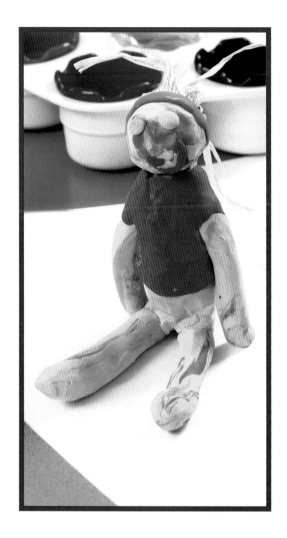

Each side of a sculpture
looks different.

What Can I Use to Make Sculptures?

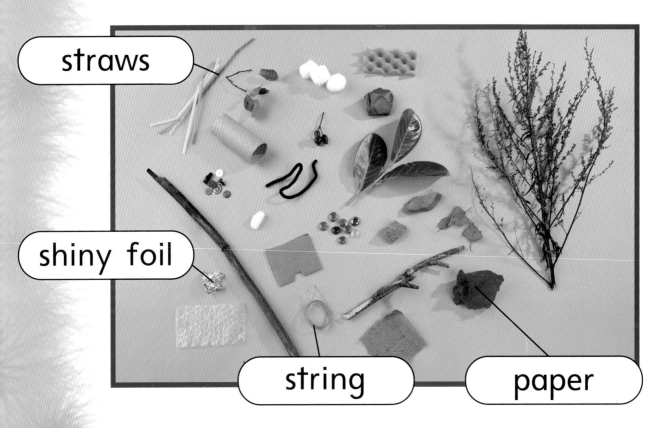

straws

shiny foil

string

paper

Look at all the **materials** you can use for sculpting.

glue

Build a model by joining things
together with glue or sticky tape.

How Can I Mak Clay and Sand Sculptures?

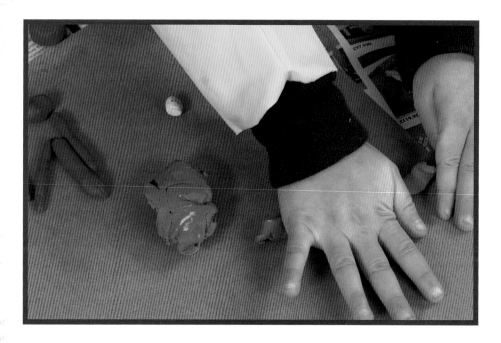

Clay is soft and squishy.

Squeeze it into shapes or roll it into strips.

Sculpting with wet sand is fun.

Decorate your sand sculptures with shells and pebbles.

How Can I Mak Paper and Cardboard Sculptures?

You can use boxes to make a model of an animal.

Draw eyes and a nose on your model.

dinosaur

Use **papier mache** to make
a dinosaur.

When your dinosaur is dry, you
can paint it.

What Can I Sculpt?

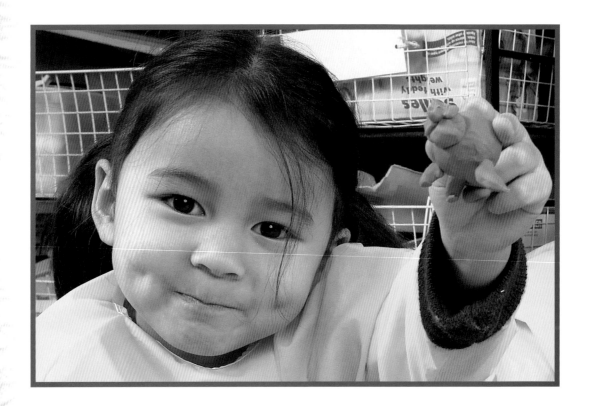

You can make a sculpture of something real, such as an animal.

You can invent a shape that is interesting to look at.

How Does Sculpting Make Me Feel?

It is fun to make art with other people.

Help each other build a big sculpture.

When you finish making a sculpture,
you feel pleased.

Let's Make a Sculpture!

Let's make a sculpture of a tree!

1. Ask a grown-up to help you collect some leaves and twigs.

2. Roll out a thick piece of clay to make the trunk. Stand it up on a board.

3. Use your fingers to make marks in the clay.

Try to make a rough **texture**, like tree bark.

4. Stick twigs and leaves into the top of the trunk.

Quiz

All these **materials** are used for sculpting.

Can you remember what they are called?

Look for the answers on page 24.

Picture Glossary

creative, page 4
making something using your own ideas
and how you feel inside

decorate, page 13
add colors and patterns to make
something look nice

material, page 10, 22
thing you use to make sculptures, such as
paper and clay

papier mache, page 15
material made of paper soaked in water
and mixed with glue

texture, page 7, 21
how something feels when you touch it

three-dimensional, page 8
shape, such as a bottle or box, that is
not flat

Note to Parents and Teachers

Reading for information is an important part of a child's literacy development. Learning begins with a question about something. Help children think of themselves as investigators and researchers by encouraging their questions about the world around them. Each chapter in this book begins with a question. Read the question together. Look at the pictures. Talk about what you think the answer might be. Then read the text to find out if your predictions were correct. Think of other questions you could ask about the topic, and discuss where you might find the answers. Assist children in using the picture glossary and the index to practice new vocabulary and research skills.

Index

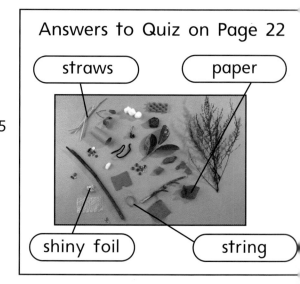

Answers to Quiz on Page 22

straws   paper

shiny foil   string